ASTONISHMENT

Titles by Anne Stevenson

ANNE STEVENSON

ASTONISHMENT

BLOODAXE BOOKS

First published 2012 by
Bloodaxe Books Ltd,
Highgreen,
Tarset,
Northumberland NE48 1RP.

www.bloodaxebooks.com
For further information about Bloodaxe titles
please visit our website or write to
the above address for a catalogue.

Supported by
**ARTS COUNCIL
ENGLAND**

Cover design: Neil Astley & Pamela Robertson-Pearce.

Printed in Great Britain by
Bell & Bain Limited, Glasgow, Scotland.

For my parents

LOUISE DESTLER STEVENSON,
1908–1963

CHARLES LESLIE STEVENSON,
1908–1979

ACKNOWLEDGEMENTS

Poems in this collection have appeared in the following newspapers and periodicals. 'The Password', 'After the Funeral' and 'Carols in King's' in *The Guardian*; 'The Loom' in *The Sewanee Review*; 'Teaching my Sons to Swim in Walden Pond', 'Doppler' and 'Paper' in *The Hudson Review*; 'Night Thoughts', 'Blackbird', 'After Words', 'How Astonishing' 'and 'Demeter and Her Daughter' were first published in *Poetry Review*, edited by Fiona Sampson. 'All Those Attempts in the Changing Room' and 'The Master and His Cast' have appeared in Michael Schmidt's *PN Review*. 'The Voice', 'Hotel New Year', 'In the Museum of Floating Bodies and Flammable Souls' and 'Drench' were first published in the *TLS*; 'On Harlech Beach' appeared in *The New Yorker* and in *Being Human*, ed. Neil Astley (Bloodaxe Books, 2011). Thanks are due to Gerry Cambridge in Scotland, who published 'Match' and 'A Visit' in *The Dark Horse*, and to the editors of *Planet* and *Poetry Wales* in Wales for publishing 'Tulips' and sections of the Ardudwy Calendar. 'Elegy: In Coherent Light' first appeared in *Gift*, a chapbook for Seamus Heaney published by Newcastle University; it subsequently appeared in *Poetry* (Chicago) as did 'The Miracle of the Bees and the Foxgloves'. 'How it is' was first published in *Poetry London*; 'Not a Hook not a Shelf, maybe a Song?' in *Other Poetry*. 'Constable Clouds and a Kestrel's Feather' was published last May in *Artemis*, edited by Myra Schneider. Special thanks go to Schlomitt Tiff, executor of Nerys Johnson's estate, for permission to use Johnson's 'Open Tulips' on the cover of this book.

Three poems in this collection – 'Photographing Change', 'In the Museum of Floating Bodies and Flammable Souls' and 'Spring' – appeared (too soon) in my Bloodaxe collection, *Poems 1955–2005*. They have all been revised and in my view improved; and since all three seemed well suited to the theme of the present collection, I decided to include them.

Finally, I must express my gratitude to several people to whom I owe an immense amount for inspiration, advice and criticism: to Angela Leighton, who read and commented on nearly every one of these poems in the course of their making; to Ian Gordon, who saw some of them into the world when he was teaching a U3A course on my work in Cambridge; and especially to Rosemary Polack, most generous of friends, who, again and again, has made my husband and myself welcome in her Cambridge home.

CONTENTS

The perpetual ideal is astonishment.

DEREK WALCOTT

Forever is composed of nows
'Tis not a different time...

EMILY DICKINSON

I

The Loom

I drowned in sleep.
And once my lungs were gills,
I watched my liquid shadow,
   fathoms deep,
Weave through a trembling warp
   of light and hope
   a weft that kills.

No working hand
Had anything to do
   with how the sea
Hurled itself in salt against the sand,
   or how unfeelingly
The shore forgot to be land
   and mimed the sea,

Or how, under the dream,
One tightening thread
Gathered those crooked strokes of light
   into a beam
Through which I rose – not quite
   from the dead –
   more from the blame

Fanned out in
Micro-shards of extinct species
   threatening my head –
Motes that might have been
   curses, or killer faces,
Had they not welcomed me, as I woke,
   with human voices.

Constable Clouds and a Kestrel's Feather

England still moulds them as Constable saw them.
We see them through his eyes –
loaves fresh kneaded for the oven,
veils of gauze,
flat-bottomed continents, creamy islands
floating on glass. As a child
did you never play the cloud-zoo game
on summer days like these?
Lie prone on grass,
stalk in your mouth, face to the sun,
to let imagination run wild
in a sky full of camels and whales
where the air show today
features fish evolving into crocodiles
disintegrating slowly
into little puffs of sheep grazing on air.
Now a tyrannosaur, chasing a bear...
or is it a white bull? Europa on his back,
panicking to disappear.

Here's a cloud that Constable never knew.
Two chalk-white furrows are being ploughed
straight as rails across the high blue
hinterland of my childhood zoo –
a plane from somewhere, going somewhere,
leaving its spoor of vapour on the air.
As the trailing furrows widen,
waves form a lingering wake from a prow
in perfect rhythm, like a feather's pattern.

And still you keep your head down,
eyes vacuuming the turf,
nose to the ground,
intent on ants and other centaurs
in their dragon world, their home
here thatched with a found

feather – evidence of hunger's habits
in this summer field.
A kestrel's, female you guess,
stroking the patterned vanes
locked to the shaft:
13 square bars, dark, on the outer side;
13 wavy lines, woven on the inner side,
a russet, bow-shaped, undesigned design
perfectly aligned – not by craft,
but by a mathematics of its own –
proof that, undeterred by our millennium,
nature's nature is to work in form.

Bird in Hand

(for Leigh Ann in Sewanee)

The tiny wren perched on your hand
could be a key. Then
somewhere should be the door
that with a bird-shaped key-hole
cut by wind into stiff sand
must fit that needle beak and pinhead eye,
that tail's armed signal to the clamped wings,
Fly! Spring the lock! Lift the floor
from the earth, the roof from the sky,
and with a fanfare of trills
– no trumpets, no veils –
reveal the Quaker heaven where this bird sings.

Teaching My Sons to Swim in Walden Pond

We must look a long time before we can see.

HENRY DAVID THOREAU

Dark woods, deep pond,
   the pond locked in the woods,
   woods looking up from the pond.
End of summer's oak-green, birch-wan,
   hickory, pitch pine, alder almost purple.
September growing skyward upside down
   in water hearsay swore was 'bottomless.'

The poet-scientist plumbed it, simple
   with fishing-line and stone:
one hundred and two feet deep, plus
   five feet not to be explained
   by inflows feeding it, outflows voiding it.
The pond was measurable.
   Its voice, immeasurable.

*

It's not so difficult to swim. Shall we begin
   our lesson in the changing room?
Off with your clothes, then: tee-shirts, jeans,
   slogans, logos, trainer socks and shoes.
Abandon your watches, music machines,
   ear pods and mobile phones.
As soon as you're fit to be fish,
   ease the weight off your bones.
Equip yourselves, scaled and finned,
     for a cool trip home.

In lesson two, spacing your bodies out,
we'll practise staying afloat.
Don't fight with feet or hands or head
your mother element.
Behave like a fallen leaf. Believe in lying down.
That's it! That's it!
Let this rock-a-bye water be your bed,
your muscles' memory, your boat.
Forget how to walk, forget to doubt.
Forget to drown.

Lesson three has to be about air,
plain air. You think it's free?
Try breathing when it isn't there.
You're sputtering. Can't speak, can't see?
Can't live without air? You'll have to save it, then.
Breathe in, breathe slowly out, breathe in,
but only when you surface. Yes!
Learn from the otter and the marsh hen
how to steal through water like grease
on a ribbon of silence.

There! How easy. Soon, with practice,
you'll be swimming – oh, not perfectly,
but maybe well enough to burrow under water,
open your eyes and see
beneath its sleepy unstoppable simmer.
Let's pretend this pond is an ancient ocean.
You have just been born.
You don't know it yet, but you're human.
The air hurts your lungs; the water hates them.
Where do you belong?

On land? In the water? In between?
    Anywhere that doesn't hurt, you say.
Pooh! Everything to do with learning hurts.
Put it another way. No creature swims
    that doesn't need to swim, except us
    who swim for fun, for play.
The mallards, the nervous little minnows, muskrats,
    frogs, even the mosquitoes and skater-bugs
belong to the pond on which their lives depend.
    Doesn't it rightfully belong to them?

Thoreau thought naming as good as owning.
    Words were for him divine currency.
Hating his neighbours' small-mindedness and greed,
    he camped in the woods, *looked* until he *saw*
    the Highest Mind made visible in Nature,
then willed America's wilderness to poetry.
    What else could it belong to after him?
    To the Indians his fathers stole it from?
To developers stripping the forest as their right?
    To Massachusetts' World Heritage Site?

Of course, Walden belongs to nature, like the trees.
But isn't everything we see in nature
    known by how we name it?
You say nature was 'better' before we splashed in,
    big heads stuffed with our own stories,
    languages to make them happen.
What if – at some road fork in evolution–
    we'd taken instead the dolphin's way?
The seal's, the otter's? We need to swim
    to keep that lost road open.

Look at the time – how late it is. Before dark,
     we'll need to put our clothes on,
pick up our picnic litter, towels and toys
     and head for the car park.
Before we do, though, turn back
     to watch the day's last hatch of insects
jet-streaming to their deaths across the pond.
     You have to hear with your eyes
to see the sunset talk with its reflection
     in those mauve gold clichés.

Now the tourists have taken their voices home,
     the crickets' thin pulsing chorus begins.
Listen to the ripples whispering to the stones.
     Thoreau would have heard them
after the hoot and rattle of the night express
     released him to the screech owls
moaning to each other across the lake like fallen souls:
     'Oh-o-o-o-o that I had never been bor-r-r-r-n!'
     With Boston already baying in the distance,
closer and louder every night, closer and fiercer.

(for Kari Furre, supreme swimmer)

20

Night Thoughts

'Love is not a hook to hang a life on.'
Who said it? Someone laughing.
Then mother in her dinner party voice
came back with, 'Well, the usual symbol
is an arrow, but that's for passion.'
(I was sitting in my nightgown on the stairs to listen.)
Then a blond falsetto man's voice almost squealed,
'Yes, Cupid's feathered fire that blinds and strips,
then leaves you naked, howling on the shingle
while Venus' shell drifts out to sea again,'
drowned in a general roar, out of which peeled
the scornful voice of my father,
'Oh, that fifteenth-century ripe vulgarity!'

And here's the book, and here's the naked lady
floating, embarrassed, on the scalloped sea.
She's hiding in a rope of golden hair.
Her sister brings her something warm to wear.

*

Who's this appearing? Why the tears?
My first piano teacher, Mrs Efron,
beloved and forgotten   sixty years

crying for lost Petersburg   lost Schumann
Kinderszenen never to return...
crying so hard I creep out from my lesson
crying. Nine years old. And yesterday.

*

Yesterday   Monday   May Bank Holiday.
Those all-but-dead crack willows by the river,
rising from trashy water in green tracery.

21

That tiny girl, her black braids flapping,
skip-roping over the puddles on the path,
skipping for the joy of skipping.

*

When tears at last drowned Julia Efron, she
forgot about teaching me to play.
For a while she stalked our upper storey,
scary at night, a shadow walking.
Waking, I heard the floorboards cry.
Then she disappeared, leaving me,
tenderly inscribed, *The Story of Painting*.

So I met and fell in love with Botticelli
whose ladies I envied for their floating clothes,
wondering at the incandescent flowery nakedness
in which they posed...

Though none were lovelier than Mrs Efron,
wishbone-thin and olive-skinned,
hair smoothed back into a coal black bun.

'And for what, except for you, do I feel love?'

She smiles at me
through tears with rainbows in them.

Paper,

the beauty of it,
the simple, strokeable, in-the-handness of it,
the way it has of flattering ink,
giving it to understand that
nothing matters
until it is printed or written down
to be cherished on paper.

The way old paper levels time,
is the archive's treasure,
is evidence talking to your fingers
when passion, two hundred years dead,
filters through the ink-net that,
pen in hand, a lover once spread for his mistress,
ignorantly scooping the archivist
into his catch.

The connoisseur of wine
keeps company with the connoisseur of paper,
as the typesetter, rag-testing, rice-testing,
escapes from the glaze of his computer
to explore with a fingertip
an elegant topography
reserved exclusively for types he likes
and faces that delight him.

All the same,
the virtual truths of the TV
and the on-going game of what happens
sluice through the global drain
in a torrent of paper.
Throw it away or save it,
every day as it dies
instantly becomes news on paper.

Why, say the silicon people,
keep house in a paper graveyard?
The future is digital, clean, indestructible,
the great web's face book and bird's nest.
No fingerprint can be lost,
no fact of identity missed.
All's for the best
in the best of all paperless worlds.

The afterlife? To live on, on line,
without a mind of one's own?
I can't love these fidgety digits!
I want to go home,
I want to keep warm in my burrow
of piled up paper –
fool's passion, dried grief, live hands of dead friends,
story I'll keep turning the pages of
until it ends.

(For Glenn Storhaug, printer,
and John Wells, archivist)

On Line

(for Harry Guest at 80)

One day, on the other side of a world war,
on the other side of an ocean, I pored over mother's
bound album of tourist snapshots – England and Italy
months before I was born – then seriously said to her,
'It must have been strange to live in the olden days
when the world was black and white without any colour.'
The scene flashed back on the East Coast line as I squeezed
into two tight feet of soiled upholstery. To my right,
a teenaged nymph hunched over an iPad; in minimal clothes,
she was scrolling for fantasy shoes. Facing me,
two smart young male laptops were open for business,
closed, of course, to the window and to England
passing outside; closed again, inside, to the pressure
of eyes, flesh and feelings inches from their screens.

In the silence of clicking keys, no one looked at me
running the sharp cardboard edge of my ticket through
the uncut pages of a rare, never-read-before *Middlemarch*,
freeing trapped pockets of breath from the 19th century –
perfectly preserved and collectable, but about as compatible
with the way we live now as trilobites with kilobytes.
What a triumph of mobile technology, the four of us
spanning three centuries in the leg room of a cell,
each on a track of our own, mine certain for the terminal,
theirs heading out into cyberspace, a New World newly
opened, fully colonised already by the dazzling young.
Do they pay, maybe, with upper-case Independence
for the luxury of lower-case instant communication,
the infallible i of the pad, the pod, the impudent phone?

Summoning the shade of my mother, I said to her,
'This is how we live in the wonderland of the future.'
'On a pea-sized, overpopulated planet,' she answered,
'in continuous communication with itself? You're welcome to it.
And why do so many of you suffer from earache?

Are you happy living this way – not hand to mouth
but conspicuously hand to ear?' My teenage neighbour
slipped me a pitying smile as she turned off the shoes
and reached for her mobile. Outside the window I watched
four jackdaws jockey for place on a tree stripped to the bone.
They took off in a flock as we passed the aborted woodland.
Sunset. A star from a gash in the fire-coloured clouds
shone bright as an eye through our ghostly reflections.
Then night gave us all, complete in ourselves, to the glass.

An Exchange in the Time Bank

I eased my life down gently on the counter
    and asked for change.
'How would you like it?' smiled the teller.
    'I'm sure we can arrange
an equable return. Will you take it in days?'
    'Summer days,' I suggested.
'Dividends in age-based percents are what the policy pays.'
    'So with my lifetime invested,
how much, say, from deposits aged three to fifteen
    will I have earned?'
'In retrievable memories?' 'Yes, that's what I mean.'
    'Well, that would depend
on how much capital you invested in childhood
    and on interest received.'
'But with bonuses in health and good luck, I should,
    with respect, have saved
quite enough in boom times to set against losses
    in depression years.'
The teller threw me a shrewd look. 'Trust us,'
    he said. 'All arrears
will be balanced faithfully once your account
    is safe on our database;
but keep in mind that corporeal rules are not about
    to be bent in your case,
nor are indemnities settled on your lifespan,
    I regret to say, renewable.
And though for senior investors we do what we can,
    it's not possible
for post-seventies savings grants to be guaranteed.'
    I eyed my old life sadly
where it lay, gazing upwards, waiting to be keyed,
    uninsured, into eternity.

'OK, I'll take it back!' He shook his head.
   'My dear, it isn't there.'
I reached, but clung to something that disintegrated,
   smoke in a puff of air,
a dream's liquidity, a failed currency,
   a mintage, surely a rarity,
valued, trusted, hoped for, ever believed in –
   volatile as money.

II

Sonnets and Variations

It's astonishing

that this is my wild left foot I'm freeing from a Lycra sock,
that these arthritic fingers once belonged to my bow hand,
slaves to a cello named Caesar and to Johann Sebastian Bach
whose solo suite Number 5 in C minor, the Sarabande,
is quietly fingering my memory: resignation and truth.
That I can lean over, flick a switch and a light will go on
surprises me, as does nodding to sleep, book in hand, and flicking it off
to revive in the dark a young cello-playing Anne Stevenson
along with strict Mr Troostewick (Troosey) in New Haven
and soft-spoken Mr Edel, feared and adored in Ann Arbor;
both by now dead, still living in their beautiful instruments. Even
Herr Haydn, Signor Boccherini, M Saint Saens and Mr Elgar,
long dead, are alive in those concertos I never quite learned to play
before I listened to my deafness. This is my left foot, poetry.

Doppler

The siren's F sharp minor drops to D,
Wailing its passage through an interface.
The traffic shifts. It's an emergency.
It's like the vacuum between air and space
When suddenly, unprepared for it, you see
The fractured pitch of your existence race
Beyond your senses to a deeper key
While still the sum of you remains in place.

The child declares, 'One day I'm going to be...'
But being is moving, moving is moving past.
The scale runs down from hope to memory,
No dream stays clear, no fantasy can last,
Feel becomes fail, and fail becomes goodbye.
If we remember otherwise, we lie.

After the Funeral

(for Sally Thorneloe, in memory of Lieutenant-Colonel Rupert Thorneloe, killed in Afghanistan, 1 July 2009)

Seeing you lost in that enormous hat,
Your face rigid with grief, I thought of how
In love with life you used to be, so much that
'Happy' seemed a word kept warm for you.
Seeing you stunned there in the camera's eye,
Forbidding your chin to undermine your lip,
I knew the knife in you was asking *why?*
And ceremony couldn't answer it,
Though they were trying desperately to give
History's unspoken underside a face,
A frame, words and a reason to believe
The afterlife is ordered – like the place
In which, beside his flag-draped coffin, you
Acted, like him, the role you'd been assigned to.

Elegy: In Coherent Light

(in memory of Matt Simpson and Michael Murphy)

Teach-cheap, teach-cheap, teach-cheap, teach-cheap –
Sparrows – plying their chisels in the summer ivy,
Chipping the seconds spark by spark out of the hours.
Each whistling chip repeats the sun's holography.
My brain's a film, I'm made of timed exposures.
Pounding my eyes and ears with waves of light,
Invisible flakes make pictures I call sight.

But now you're out of the picture, no one can keep
Coherent track of you, except in language.
All the warm rhetoric is wrong. Death isn't sleep.
Faith in eternal love is love's indulgence.
I prize what you wrote, meet you in what I write,
Still keep house in our crumbling tenement of words.
Pull down their walls of ivy, and you kill the birds.

The Miracle of the Bees and the Foxgloves

Because hairs on their speckled daybeds baffle the little bees,
Foxgloves hang their shingles out for rich bumbling hummers,
Who crawl into their tunnels-of-delight with drunken ease
(See Darwin's pages on his foxglove summers)
Plunging over heckles caked with sex-appealing stuff,
To sip from every hooker an intoxicating liquor
That stops it propagating in a corner with itself.

And this is how the foxglove keeps its sex life in order.
Two anthers – adolescent, in a hurry to dehisce –
Let fly too soon, so pollen lies in drifts about the floor.
Along swims bumbler bee and makes an undercoat of this,
Reverses, exits, lets it fall by accident next door.
So ripeness climbs the bells of *Digitalis* flower by flower,
Undistracted by a mind, or a design, or by desire.

The Master and His Cast

A tribute to Henry James

Passing first class on their luxury liner through the straits
of the nineteenth and twentieth centuries, they lingered on deck
in dinner jackets and jewelled gowns, looking perhaps like advertisements
for expensive perfume, but playing for possession of the sunset.
Fortunes steamed over the sea to them, waiters in black raced between them
bearing trays of iced syrup and soda-water, while at ease
in the narrows of their ways, he steered them through a channel of lawns
green as billiard tables, shaded by porticos and elm trees –
beauty at its cruellest most civilised at Matcham and Fawns.
Justice settled which girls would be turned into monsters,
which would suffer victory to vindicate innocence. Yes, wealth
does a great deal to worry goodness in those late, magniloquent chapters,
more art than odyssey, more parable than myth;
and why should a gilded tour of betrayal not feature privilege and princes?
Beyond the next rock lay the wreck. It moves me to think of him
scrupulously analysing Scylla right there on the lip of Charybdis.

Not a Hook, not a Shelf, maybe a Song?

'Love is too frail a hook to hang a life on.'
After the thrills of Ecstasy or booze,
The rites of hymen meet the wrongs of women,
And love begins to ease loose from its screws.

Becomes a shelf to raise a family on –
Love on a mortgage and a nine-to-five
Wearing away in blameless repetition,
The telly, Tesco's, kids, a four-wheel-drive.

So where is love? Love is the under-chorus.
Everyone knows it, beats it, hums it, *Luv*
As it should have been and maybe sometimes was.
I hope it's love these shopping faces dream of,

Hungry Miss Pink Hair with her iPod ear;
Sad Mrs Pushchair, pregnant every year.

How it is

The old stone streets of Durham are losing their cobbles like teeth.
On they drill, those big shouldered County-Council blokes
in pit hats and yellow jackets, ear-splitting stone-splitters cordoned off
to prise up time's suppurating slag and lay down new time in fresh rocks.
But time is space, and the paving they pound in is never so heavy
as the air they work in. It's not even air that's wrinkling them into
grey twists of men smoking outside the hospital doors after coronary
scares, or bodies wheeled through fluorescent corridors, gazing at you
in astonishment, grateful for the latest in hip replacements.
Tick tock go the secretaries' heels, statistics in command
checking out the wards. Nurses glide by, their professional competence
neutered by brogues and uniforms, raised drips in hand.
Everyone is being taken care of, don't worry, you will be all right,
say the men in green fatigues, removing their gloves and mouth masks.
Screens are still talking brightly when the theatres close for the night,
but it's hard to believe you're the blokes you thought you were,
> and no one asks.

The Voice

The ancient belief that body lets go its ghost
Only at death, like invisible thistledown – no!
I'd sooner believe the opposite is so,
That flesh is the flyaway guest a spacious host
Breathes in and out, an element at most
That in transmission clings and starts to grow,
Nameless today, tomorrow a face, a show,
Parented, schooled, determinedly self-engrossed,
Till eyes' exchanges seem reliable,
And 'Here I am!' agrees with 'We have seen.'
A few, though, slip behind the human screen,
Where what they meet's so wonder-terrible
They never dare pretend again they've been
More than a voice in the void, a link between.

Caring More Than Caring

(to Dewi Stephen Jones)

So, we will not meet, we'll never sit
Filling in the silence, smiling bravely,
Chatting about the weather, sipping tea,
As if time's passing mattered not a bit
And age's roughcast could be faced with wit.
Nothings will not be handed on politely,
To lighten hours that otherwise might be
Heavy with language caring won't admit.

My not visiting, your not wanting me –
What could bring us closer to understanding
The unsaid rules of truth in poetry?
Not playing well is sometimes more demanding
Than playing to win, where winning would be lying,
Where losing is a kind of setting free.

Carols in King's

Life, like a dome of many-coloured glass,
Stains the white radiance of Eternity.

Flooding the winter grass,
    making ice of the chapel walls,
        the moon through many-coloured glass

appeared in intervals
    of many-coloured air;
        though, with the lights and cameras

all focused elsewhere –
    on the jubilant hosannas
        of the choir, and in the nave,

on lined, self-conscious faces –
    few thought that spotlight from above
        was more exalted than their voices

or saw how the chapel had become
    in moonlight
        Shelley's human-coloured dome.

(for Rosemary Polack)

III

Ardudwy

Wind from the North,
Crouch by the hearth.

Wind from the East,
Roar of the beast.

Wind from the South,
A kiss on the mouth.

Wind from the West,
Rain and unrest.

Night Snow

Fallen   more white flags falling.
Truce between all and nil.

White feathers plucked free of their wings,
white wings without justifying angels.

Still falling steadily, silently –
return of the simplified dead.

White is the valency colour,
touching, embracing all colour.

Not even the night sky is negative.
Turn up your face for its kiss.

Under the whiteness, a blackness
readying itself to be greenness.

Gaia, fast sleep in her wedding shroud,
warming her genes for resurrection.

Thaw

I've pulled back the curtain
to look at the day,
stale already from its dull incubation
in yesterday and the day before.
Sodden melt for a garden.
A sour milk sky.
How alike they are.
The light spreads now
as the sun sweats into it –
a clutch of forgotten sweets
gone soft in their sticky paper.

Spring Diary
(for Rhian Samuel)

Arrival Dream

Walking by an open window in a foreign city.
Out of it flies, like a letter through a slot, a burst of laughter.
Something to pick up and keep for a souvenir.
I can't read the language.
The youthful look of that green and yellow stamp.

Snow Squalls

When spring comes, winter succumbs,
furiously hurling its sequins at the young sun.
Spoiled petals. Not yet defeated daffodils.
Gwilym seeding with newborn lambs
the unchanged hills.

North Easter

It happens every day and night,
    the weather in Wales,
fluting through window-cracks and keyholes,
spinning round and around the Cwm,
    an old dog turning in its basket.

Spring, with its killer instinct,
    keeps a strangle-hold on the year.
Through scrims of industrial air,
    the mountains recede – heaps of Mabinogion scenery.
Don't expect Branwyn or Pryderi to appear.

Even that keeled-over ash I used to see
    as the wing of a crashed angel
has the look of abandoned fantasy.

Wind batters it down in one way,
    then beats it again, and again
        in the same way.

A Clearer Memory

Every spring renews the blackbird for me
just when he claims the season for himself,
as out of the deep well of his voice I heft,
with a longer rope, a clearer memory.

Then, like a present,

two weeks of dry wind – joy for the jackdaws –
sweeping the air with haze and chaffinches.
The old house complains... those aching doors.
Mud becomes dust in the ditches.
Summer has locked up its hostile barometers.
Light cleans protesting corners with dirty fingers.

*   *   *

On Harlech Beach

Sharpen your eyes looking back from the tide's headland,
and the Lowry figures on the beach could be movable type –
a *p*, pink, *i*, indigo, an *x* running yellow and tan
in pursuit of a flying stop. What an alphabet soup
the bay makes of them, these large fathered families
downloading their daughters and sons, sans serif and
sans grief, on the centrefold page of the sand.

From which a Welsh double *l* is detaching itself –
lovers, hand-linked by a hyphen, weaving with ease
through the ins and outs of the waves' parentheses.
From a distance how simple they look, how picturesque.
Three dots (an ellipsis in action) rush back and forth –
terriers seeking, retrieving, time-free and carefree
as only dogs in illiterate joyousness can be.

It's a scene to write about. You could walk back
cheering – if not for the human story, for the display
it offers to the pattern-hungry eye –
the body sway of the lovers, a Frisbee caught
by a bronze torso, striped pigments of cloud and sky
brushed by an appearing, disappearing sun;
prone golden mums and their lucky cartwheeling young.

As if this were a playground raised from the dead for them,
the salvaged remains of old beachheads, suffered and won.
Unremarked by the holiday crowd, two faraway swarms –
I would paint them as shadows in khaki and bloodstained brown –
turn out to be birds: an invasion of scavenging *m*'s
whose squabble of laughter is raucous enough to drown
those boys shouting *King of the castle* as they kick it down.

Drench

You sleep with a dream of summer weather,
wake to the thrum of rain – roped down by rain.
Nothing out there but drop-heavy feathers of grass
and rainy air. The plastic table on the terrace
has shed three legs on its way to the garden fence.
The mountains have had the sense to disappear.
It's the Celtic temperament – wind, then torrents, then remorse.
Glory rising like a curtain over distant water.
Old stonehouse, having steered us through the dark,
docks in a pool of shadow all its own.
That widening crack in the gloom is like good luck.
Luck, which neither you nor tomorrow can depend on.

On Reflection

(to John Redmond)

That fire in the garden's an illusion –
the double of the fire that warms this room.
Now standing at the window in between them,
I watch the spiked montbretia blaze in bloom
and guess the glass is telling me a lie.
But no, the flames are there. I can't deny
the evidence presented to my eye.
That's why it's to my doubt I must appeal
for news of what is false and what is real.

October Song

Don't ask the beech tree why the season is
Rusting with the bracken in the marsh.
Let be the finches at their thistly feed.
The tired leaves singly drifting from the birch
Can have no inkling what the reason is,
Or why it is the thorniest bushes bleed
In red haw, hip and rowanberry weather,
When little patchwork quilts of gorse and heather
Fade in the glister of the spider's stitch.

Will this be the last day? Or this? Or this?
After this winter, will I see another?

Goat Cull in Cwm Nancol

You, Mr Crow,
where are you flying to?
Over the tawny marsh,
over the craggy fell.
Why is your voice so harsh,
casting your spell,
casting your hungry spell?
Mr Crow, don't call on me.

You, little goat,
where has your mammy gone?
Yesterday I spied a man.
He was a stranger on your hill,
stalking with his clever gun
and itch to kill.
Run, little goat, when you spy me, run!
That man was me.

Roses in December

Two small unofficial footnotes.
One red asterisk
argues with the rust on the fence
topping our wall.
One afterthought, prickly with quotes,
adds bright evidence
to a tangle of still-green periwinkle.

Another spring
– even an age of intelligence –
may still be possible.

IV

Photographing Change

*(to Ernestine Rubin, Steve Coll
and Carrie Hitchcock, photographers)*

How can it be that empty, intangible age
        is stronger than we are?
Fuelled by the sun, time sky-writes *begin here*
on the eastern right hand corner
        of a turning page
every morning when, expectantly awake,
we use up hours that taste and feel alike.
        So why are days so differently
the same? Think, days will happen after you
and I no longer need to plan them sensibly,
        or bring to mind a few
urgent forgettable things we have to do.

Think, too, of the split second when a finger
        triggers a snapshot,
shooting time dead. Only when it can't
recur can 'that wonderful day' be caught
        on sepia flypaper.
So the old rapscallion visits his wedding
fifty years after the marriage ended in
        pained, unphotographed divorce.
And the dressed up smiling guests don't know,
        of course,
how long they'll be arrested for. 'That's ... who?'
'I can't remember what her name was now.'

An unwinnable game, then. Keep the surface,
  lose the name,
or lose both by attending to the stream
that hurls them onward at the same
  irreversible pace.
Try photographing change. Try stones, try
trees. Bearded with lichen, they are streaming by,
  free of Plato's petrified ideal.
One wave laps into another. The foam-white
struggle of the brook is its appeal.
Let a river be invented by a stroke of light
that anneals it as it vanishes from sight.

In the Museum of Floating Bodies and Flammable Souls

(for Angela Leighton)

Painters who painted the flights of martyrs for money,
Who filled the drapery of saints with rose-tinted oil,
Had to please rich patrons with trapeze acts of the body,
Since no one can paint the electricity of the soul.

My lady in her blue silk cowl must by now be topsoil;
She swans into Heaven, almond eyes uplifted in piety.
My lord kneels at prayer in a cassock, blade at his heel;
Not a single cell of him sings of his wealth and charity.

While in Hell – well preserved in the water church of Torcello –
The wicked receive their deserts. Disembowelled or dismembered,
They are set upon eternally, yet their bodies alone are touched;
Unless souls flushed out of the flesh are the flames that torch them.

No wonder evil is interesting and goodness pitifully dull.
Torture of the body symbolises torture of the mind,
Though burning in the bonfires of conscience is hardly confined
To a hell for bad Italians – saved by being damned so well.

All Those Attempts in the Changing Room

A discourse of Rembrandt van Rijn

Look for me
where I learned to look for myself,
in my ring of attempts
in the light of a sinking candle.

A candle?

      My soul, if you will.
My paintings bear witness to its
long affair with the real.
My flesh preferred games and counterfeits.

Counterfeits?

      My portraits!
The diary I kept in pigments.
This youthful 'me' – one instance –
in a beret and swaggering chain.
The sneer on my lips?
      That's envy spurring ambition.
The gold of my cheek and chin?
      There's the cost of pretence.

So I played to the glass,
desiring the sweets of applause,
every morning delivered my face
to a rasher cause:
      van Rijn, the actor, the lover,
      the courtier, the beggar,
      the burgher, the sinner,
      the saint, the seducer...

The more lies I told under cover
the truer they were.

God save me! My pictures, whatever my will,
told the truth to my eyes!

And that was your genius.

My *ingenium*? Christ's punishing muscle!
God was always at war with my skill.

With your skill?

More likely the Devil.
Oh, my struggles with God
rivalled Jacob's with the angel.
Even as a young man, I knew where I stood:
Here was God. Here was Satan.
I prayed to them both, damned both,
took from both when I could.

From Lucifer, light – ochre bronze and lead-white.
A fine brush for elegance – linen and gold –
His greed to paint glory and splendour in firelight –

But from the Lord God, eyes.

And when He handed me eyes,
I knew I'd never escape them.
I shrunk them, I botched them again and again
in the shade of my hair or my hat.
I surrounded my forehead with shadows,
wore black and more black.

But my eyes still insist that I judge
myself through them –
myself in the changing room of myself,
myself in Act One on the world's stage,
my root nose – lecherous, cruel, pocked, thick,
my smooth skin bared for the plague,
myself who would see myself mocked in old age,
poor, unrepentant, penniless ... sick, sick!

Self-portrait as a young man?

Ignorant, egotistical, clever young man.
Who could know then
what I'd be in years to come?
Or what eventually did or must happen?

Tulips

For my birthday you've brought me tulips.
I want them to fan from a low vase.
This green and white one with a cracked glaze
almost the shape of a bulb looks right.

*

Tulips were bursting from that same pot
on the same day in New York... maybe 1958.
Twenty-five tulips instead of twenty-five candles,
and we dined by tulip light.

*

There is always another war, but
these tall disciplined redcoats
have lost the battle.
Cut down, shipped alive into exile,
for nearly a week they bleed upright.

*

Two artists: this one, who catches
the incendiary character of tulips
with daring panache.
Now this one, who uses his brush
like hawks' eyesight.

*

When Nerys in her wheelchair painted tulips
they were strawberry-coloured, like her hair.
She gave them a life far longer
than the one life gave her.
When 'nature imitates art', nature
sometimes loses the fight.

*

Old tulips, getting ready to die,
swan on their wondering necks away
from their source in mother water,
obsessed with an airy faith in light.

*

These sad women in mauve – making up for
painted wrinkles with pinker hair –
drunkenly spill themselves over the bar.
Lips, lips, without love or appetite.

*

But look. At the core of each flower,
a black star,
a hope-pod, a love-seed
the seminal colour of night.

(Remembering Nerys Johnson, painter)

The Password

Memory, intimate camera, inward eye,
Open your store, unlock your silicon
And let my name's lost surfaces file by.
What password shall I type to turn you on?

Is this the girl who bicycled to school,
A cello balanced on her handlebars?
Shy, but agog for love, she played the fool
And hid her poems in the dark of drawers.

First love of music bred a love of art,
Then art a love of actors and their plays,
Then actors love of acting out a part,
Until she'd try on anything for praise.

Siphoned to England, she embraced her dream,
With Mr Darcy camped in Hammersmith,
Bathed in a kitchen tub behind a screen,
Pretending love was true and life a myth.

Waking with a baby on her hip,
Yeats in her shopping basket, here she is,
Thin as a blade and angry as a whip,
Weighing her gift against her selfishness.

Three husbands later, here she is again,
Fighting her own defiance, breaking rules.
Not mad, not microwaved American,
She trips on sense, and falls between two stools,

Finding herself at sixty on the floor,
With childhood's sober, under-table view
Of how in time love matters more and more.
Given a creeping deadline, what to do?

Look at the way her wild pretensions end.
One word, its vast forgiving coverage,
Validates all her efforts to defend
Every excuse she makes and warms with age.

Five Poems in Memory of a Marriage

A Match

Lashing a matchbox with a match, he freed a golden flame,
    then lit her cigarette before his, like a gentleman.
It was their champagne-sipping wedding night, but all the same
    he put the match back in the box – it was his party game –
    quipping, 'That was a good one. Let's save it to use again.'

After Words

'Having lived long and softly
   in the office of my head
with its rules to scold me,
   I didn't know I was unhappy
until you said... I said...
   when my tears told me.'

Hotel New Year

Tears on the windowpane
      for times we were living through.
In every drop, a grief
      that would be forgotten.

Fireworks lighting the new
      from the glowing butt of the old.

The glittering slime of the tarmac.
      Poisoned rain.
Arc lights draining the deserted
      seaside fun fair.
Dead leaves, litter, a thrown-away
      greasy condom.

When did the heartbeat stop
      in the long case clock?

Epitaph for a Hedonist

A gay blade in the happy sense of gay,
He dared to risk and risked all to enjoy.
He changed his wives but never changed his way,
And as a man, remained the winsome boy.

A Visit

In a dream you came to me
just as you used to be,
cocky, handsome,
smooth without a beard,
though hardly self-assured
as you appeared,
having, as you confessed,
lost all your money.

Somewhere on my messy desk
were the intimate records
of our joint income.
Yes, here was a file
of tattered yellow strips
heaped neatly next to me,
morphing into the Chance pile
in Monopoly.
And here was the boot,
the lovely Lagonda, the hat,
the luxury liner.
Why did I always choose the boot,
and you the boat or the car?
And how had these cards
cut out for clever children
turned into paying-in-slips?
I stared at the lucky million
printed in Ariel Bold
on every one.

Just as I thought' I said,
You're rich!' 'No, just old' –
lightly admitted,
as rueful, maybe surprised,
you shook your head.

I woke up when I realised
that every delectable moment
your daring had won you
or earned you had been well spent.
You weren't unhappy, dead.

* * *

Demeter and Her Daughter

Demeter speaks:

Just at the worst time, May!
I was teaching my ignorant soils
How to manage the flowers,
So was looking another way
When the silly girl tripped on the coils
Of ophidian Nether Powers,
And the bastard bore her away.

In my fury in June and July,
I punished the grass.
I wrung the clouds dry of their rain
And let the flowers die.
I ordered the sun as he passed
To burn the collaborative grain;
Then I stormed him out of the sky!

Well, he told me where she had gone,
Even cannoned a shaft for me –
A filthy hole – to the land
Where tubers and roots are born.
And there sat Persephone
With that criminal hand in hand
On a mound of dung like a throne.

Is that you, mother?' she cried,
Fuck off! Don't bother me here,
This is *my* space!
Can't you be satisfied
Bossing two thirds of the year
From your own high place
Without grafting me to your side?'

You watch your language,' I said,
Controlling myself. The foul air
Stank of bitumen,
It was damp as a urinal there.
When I saw that my child had died
While not yet fully a woman,
I broke down and cried.

How do you think they responded?
They laughed! They fancied a joint!
They pointedly smoked *my* weed
Entwined on their dungy bed –
Until, in astonishment,
They watched every tear I shed
Become a seed, each seed

Branch into a stem,
Dicotyledon at first
But in seconds a creeping bramble,
Beneath, before, behind them,
As a desert becomes a jungle
After a cloudburst.
I told that miracle to bind them,

Forgetting the offending oaf
Hades, as he used to be,
Or Pluto – pick your nomenclature –
Was also a god, my brother
Who splits my heritage with me.
There in the bowels of the earth
He held the hegemony.

So my thorny lianas weakened
In that tunnelled air.
Starved of celestial energy,
They peaked and sickened,
Flopped back like filthy hair –
Now worms, now whips, now graffiti,
Now *son et lumière*.

Then mud hot as hangover sweat
Oozed out of a cave
Composted with glittering slime.
The place was a communal grave
Where Death, in his element,
Stirs into compact time,
My hideous nourishment.

Oh, how had my beautiful darling –
Under age, anorexic, depressed –
Become his queen?
Now listen, because in the telling
This story – a myth at best –
At its tabloid worst has been
Skewed by corrupt reporting.

I insist that the truth be told.
Hades grows no fruit.
That over-sold pomegranate
Was indigestible gold.
Persephone never touched it.
All she ate was one shrivelled
Loganberry, grey with mould.

But it tasted of my tears.
So she upped stakes and came to me
In a sort of daze.
Maybe for the first time in years,
She considered her ways.
Maybe she was hungry
Or needed to wash her clothes.

Whatever it was, she chose
To walk out on her lover
Without a word of apology.
Their affair, it seems, was over,
Though, knowing how the world goes,
I supposed the split was temporary.
Thank goodness, it was.

For once Persephone was home,
She couldn't live a day with me
Without a quarrel.
Spring came, grain grew, sun shone,
Buds flowered. She hated us all.
At last, dying to be alone,
I set her free.

When, one rainy day in October,
She was gone, I was almost glad.
She did nothing but smoke,
Mope and be rude
When I tried to talk to her.
I love her. I knew she'd come back.
As she still does, summer after summer.

Ye unjust gods, I've tried!
I can't get through to her.
I've always been faithful and dignified,
And she's – well, a slut.
Everything ugly appeals to her,
She loves her muck.
The future is hers to decide.

Spring Again

A touch of blue
in the look of the air –
that tangy, Mozartian

unsuspicious colour.
Naïve light rounding a
steel-scrubbed corner.

Wide-open beech tree,
bare still,
pregnant with flower.

Who can believe a
summer will relieve
this undernourished hour?

Between Mersh and Averil,
When spray beginneth to springe,
The lutel fowl hath hire wil...

Though the elm's low bough
that should be in leaf
is not here now.

The thrush is gone
from the brushwood sheaf,
and that blackened thorn

is a rack of hooks
with plastic sacks
to hang wet weather in.

For all that's wrong,
Lenten is come with love to towne.
New times, old words.

In a light green haze,
let's try, with the practical birds,
to praise love's ways.

NOTES

Constable Clouds and a Kestrel Feather (14)
'ants and other centaurs ...' echoes Ezra Pound's famous line 'The ant's a centaur in his dragon world' from the *Pisan Cantos*.

Teaching My Sons to Swim in Walden Pond (17)
The title was conceived in 1970 when, as a fellow of the Bunting Institute at Harvard, I did begin to teach my sons, then four and five, to swim in the Pond. This poem, written in 2009, is hardly the poem I failed to write then, though my concern for the fate of Thoreau's 'Nature' is the same. '*Oh-o-o-o-o that I had never been born*' quotes from Thoreau's *Walden*, Chapter 4, 'Sounds'.

Night Thoughts (21)
'And for what, except for you do I feel love?': from Wallace Stevens, 'Notes Toward a Supreme Fiction', *Collected Poems* (Faber & Faber, 1959), p. 380.

Section II: Sonnets and Variations
The ten sonnets included here range from exercises in straight iambic pentameter to experiments with metrical irregularities and with extending the normal 14 to 16 lines – in one case breaking the lines up into threes, *à la* William Carlos Williams. Where the form is more regular, I have set an upper-case letter at the beginning of each line in the traditional way; where irregular I have followed the practice of free verse and written the lines as sentences. I have taken pains, however, to keep rhyme and stress-beats pretty well within the bounds of Hopkins' 'sprung rhythm' – that is, allowing no more than three unstressed syllables to separate stressed ones and giving to English sound-phrases their full measure of speech time. However, taking as a model conventional musical notation, I have sometimes allowed two (stressed) crotchets to be divided into four (unstressed) quavers or even eight equivalent semi-quavers. Sonnets such as 'The Master and His Cast' should be read as if accented in bars, like music, not as prosodic feet or by counting syllables.

Elegy: In Coherent Light (33)
In 2009, the gifted Anglo-Irish poet, Michael Murphy, died aged 44 of a brain tumour. His friend, the Liverpool poet, Matt Simpson, died only a few months later after an unsuccessful bypass operation. Both are profoundly missed today.

coherent *adj.* 4. Physics. (of two or more waves) having the same frequency and the same phase or fixed phase difference: *coherent light.* (Collins Dictionary of the English Language).

holography *n.* the practice of exposing a film to light reflected from an object or objects and to a beam of coherent light; when the patterns on the film are illuminated by the coherent light a three dimensional image (a **hologram**) is produced. (Collins, *ibid.*)

'Every bit of a hologram contains information about the whole scene, so you can snip it to pieces and [in each piece] see the original scene...' (*The Observer*, 15 May, 1966, quoted in *OED*).

The Miracle of the Bees and the Foxgloves (34)
In seven pages of *The Effects of Cross- and Self-Fertilisation in the Vegetable Kingdom* (London, 1876), 81-88, Charles Darwin describes an experiment he began in June 1869 among the foxgloves at Caerdeon above the Mawddach estuary, a half day's walk across the hills from Pwllymarch (see Ardudwy below). This was just one of his thousands of experiments demonstrating the superiority of cross-fertilisation and throwing light on the origin of sexuality.

The Master and His Cast (35)
Matcham and Fawns are country estates in James' late novel, *The Golden Bowl*. In classical mythology there are several conflicting accounts of Scylla, a beautiful girl turned by a jealous Circe into a hideous sea-monster who preyed on sailors from one coast of the straits of Messina, while the whirlpool Charybdis wrecked their ships on the other. Henry James, creator of anti-heroines such as Charlotte Stant and Kate Croy, died in 1916, believing (correctly) that with the First World War the high European civilisation he prized had come to an end.

Ardudwy (41)
An ancient district of Gwynedd, North Wales where my husband and I spend months every year in our cottage, Pwllymarch in Cwm Nantcol, shown on the cover of *Poems 1955–2005* (Bloodaxe Books, 2005). The five lyrics of 'Spring Diary' have been set for voice and accompanying instruments by the Welsh composer Rhian Samuel.

Goat Cull in Cwm Nantcol (51)
Every year in late autumn, an official cull of feral goats takes place in hills of Cwm Nantcol. Professional marksmen, contracted by the Countryside Council for Wales, locate and kill family groups of nannies,

yearlings and kids until a set quota is completed. In difficult terrain, the corpses are left where they fell as carrion for the crows and ravens. Apart from humans, wild goats have no natural predators.

All Those Attempts in the Changing Room (57)
This poem could not have been written without constant recourse to Simon Schama's magnificent study, *Rembrandt's Eyes* (London: Allen Lane, Penguin Books, 1999).

Tulips (60)
Nerys Johnson, in whose memory this poem was written, was a painter whose 'psychological' studies of flowers, especially tulips, became symbols of her brave survival and victory in a life-long struggle with rheumatoid arthritis. She died in 2001. Her paintings are reproduced on the covers of both this book and my earlier collection *Granny Scarecrow*.

Spring Again (74)
The passages in italics are verses from anonymous lyrics of the 13th century. See W.H. Auden and Norman Holmes Pearson, eds., *Poets of the English Language*, Vol. I (New York: The Viking Press, 1950), pp. 24 and 22.

Anne Stevenson was born in Cambridge, England, in 1933, of American parents, and grew up in New England and Michigan. She studied music, European literature and history at the University of Michigan, returning later to read English and write the first critical study of Elizabeth Bishop. After several transatlantic switches, she settled in Britain in 1964, and has since lived in Cambridge, Scotland, Oxford, the Welsh Borders and latterly in North Wales and Durham.

She has held many literary fellowships, and was the inaugural winner of Britain's biggest literary prize, the Northern Rock Foundation Writer's Award, in 2002. In 2007 she was awarded three major prizes in her native USA: the $200,000 Lannan Lifetime Achievement Award for Poetry by the Lannan Foundation of Santa Fe, a Neglected Masters Award from the Poetry Foundation of Chicago and The Aiken Taylor Award in Modern American Poetry from *The Sewanee Review* in Tennessee. In 2008, The Library of America published Anne Stevenson: *Selected Poems*, edited by Andrew Motion, in conjunction with the Neglected Masters Award. This series is exclusively devoted to the greatest figures in American literature.

As well as her numerous collections of poetry, Anne Stevenson has published a biography of Sylvia Plath (1989), a book of essays, *Between the Iceberg and the Ship* (1998), and two critical studies of Elizabeth Bishop's work, most recently *Five Looks at Elizabeth Bishop* (Bloodaxe Books, 2006). Her latest poetry books are *Poems 1955-2005* (2005), *Stone Milk* (2007) and *Astonishment* (2012), all from Bloodaxe. *Astonishment* is a Poetry Book Society Recommendation.